Drake and Daphne Make a Discovery

Story by

Renée Vajko Srch

Illustrated by

Faythe Payol

Drake and Daphne Make a Discovery by Renée Vajko Srch

Copyright © 2020. All rights reserved.

ALL RIGHTS RESERVED: No part of this book may be reproduced, stored, or transmitted, in any form, without the express and prior permission in writing of Pen It! Publications. This book may not be circulated in any form of binding or cover other than that in which it is currently published.

  This book is licensed for your personal enjoyment only. All rights are reserved. Pen It! Publications does not grant you rights to resell or distribute this book without prior written consent of both Pen It! Publications and the copyright owner of this book. This book must not be copied, transferred, sold or distributed in any way.

  Disclaimer: Neither Pen It! Publications, or our authors will be responsible for repercussions to anyone who utilizes the subject of this book for illegal, immoral or unethical use.

  This is a work of fiction. The views expressed herein do not necessarily reflect that of the publisher.

  This book or part thereof may not be reproduced in any form, stored in a retrieval system, or transmitted in any form by any means-electronic, mechanical, photocopy, recording or otherwise-without prior written consent of the publisher, except as provided by United States of America copyright law.

Published by Pen It! Publications, LLC in the U.S.A.
812-371-4128   www.penitpublications.com

ISBN: 978-1-954868-11-3

Illustrated by Faythe Payol

This Book Belongs To

_____

Dedication

To my sister, Gail.

Thank you for your love and support.

Two little ducks set out one day,

down to the pond to swim and play.

"What a beautiful day," said Drake.

"Yes, it is," Daphne agreed.

"It's perfect weather for a swim."

"Good morning, Drake and Daphne!" Holly the horse neighed, as the ducks waddled past.

"Where are you two going on such a lovely day?"

"We're going for a swim," Daphne quacked.

"Down by the pond," Drake added.

"Would you like to come with us?"

"No, thank you," Holly said.

"Galloping is much more fun for me."

With a *neigh*, she dashed off, her thick brown mane flowing behind her.

"I wish I could gallop like Holly," Daphne quacked.

Drake nodded. "Me too. Isn't she lovely?"

Then he had an idea. "Why don't we give it a try?"

The two little ducks slid under the fence and ran after the horse, waddling as fast as they could. But their legs were too short and their feet too flat.

With a *thud*, the ducks fell to the ground.

Daphne hung her head. "I don't think I'll ever be able to gallop like Holly."

"Me neither," sighed Drake.

The two little ducks dusted themselves off, said goodbye to Holly, then went on their way.

"Good morning, Drake and Daphne!" Penelope the pig oinked, as the ducks waddled past. "Where are you two going on such a lovely day?"

"We're going for a swim," Daphne quacked.

"Down by the pond," Drake added. "Would you like to come with us?"

"No, thank you," Penelope said. Rolling in the mud is much more fun for me."

With an *oink,* the pig sank into the thick, ooey-gooey mud, snuffling as she rolled back and forth.

"I wish I could roll in the mud like Penelope," Daphne quacked.

Drake nodded. "Me too. She looks so happy."

Then he had an idea. "Why don't we give it a try?"

The two little ducks followed Penelope into the mud.

But their legs were too short and the mud too thick.

Soon, they were stuck in the ooey-gooey muck.

Splish, splosh.

Daphne frowned. "I don't think I'll ever enjoy rolling in the mud like Penelope."

"Me neither," sighed Drake.

The two little ducks cleaned themselves off, said goodbye to Penelope, then went on their way.

"Good morning, Drake and Daphne!" Hattie the hen clucked, as the ducks waddled past. "Where are you two going on such a lovely day?"

"We're going for a swim," Daphne quacked.

"Down by the pond," Drake added. "Would you like to come with us?"

"No, thank you," Hattie said. "Roosting is much more fun for me."

With a *cluck*, the hen flew up to the coop, gripping the perch firmly with her claws. She fluffed her feathers then tucked her head under her wing and went to sleep.

"I wish I could roost like Hattie," Daphne quacked.

Drake nodded. "Me too. She looks so peaceful."

Then he had an idea. "Why don't we give it a try?"

The two little ducks flew up to the roost. But their feet were too flat to grip the perch.

Slowly, they slid down, down, down, and toppled to the ground with a *thump*.

Daphne scowled. "I don't think I'll ever be able to roost like Hattie."

"Me neither," sighed Drake.

The two little ducks shook out their feathers, said goodbye to Hattie, then went on their way.

When they reached the pond, they slid into the water, their little webbed feet paddling beneath the surface as they glided across the water.

"Mom!" they heard a little girl squeal by the shore. "Watch those ducks. Aren't they lovely?"

"They certainly are," the mother said. "They look so happy and peaceful."

Daphne looked at Drake and smiled.

"I guess it's okay not to be like Holly, Penelope, or Hattie, because I'm perfect just being me."

The End

About the Author

Born to an American father and a British mother, Renée Vajko Srch grew up in France where she obtained her French Baccalaureate. She attended IBME in Switzerland, graduating with a degree in Theology. She is a speaker with Stars for Autism, educating and training individuals and businesses about autism.

She currently lives in the Missouri Ozarks with her husband and three sons. She is a connoisseur of fine chocolates, an avid reader, and has a weakness for rescue cats.

Renée is a staff-writer for Herald and Banner Press. Several of her articles have been published in the Missouri Autism Report magazine. Two of her stories have been published in *Chicken Soup for the Soul* books and aired on two different podcasts. She also authors a blog on autism, motherhood and God. She is currently working on her second novel as well as a devotional for autism and special needs families.

You can follow her on Facebook (Author Renée Vajko Srch, Twitter (Renee Srch@SrchRenee), Pinterest (MotherhoodAutismAndGod), and Instagram (ReneeVajkoSrch).

Follow the author at: www.reneevajkosrch.com

About the Illustrator
Faythe Payol

Born to American missionaries in Zaire, Faythe's family fled from the rebels to France where she was raised. She obtained her Baccalaureate at the American School of Paris, attended Philadelphia College of the Bible for two years, then transferred to Huntington College in Indiana graduating with a Bachelor's degree, majoring in Art.

As a professional awarded-artist, Faythe has spent many years painting and selling her Art work in the heart of Paris where she is a member of the *Peintres du Marais*.

She teaches English, Visual Arts, and coordinates art shows for the students at the American School of Paris.

Loving mother and caring grandmother, Faythe and her husband Francis currently live in France where they enjoy spending time discovering the wonders of the countryside in Britany.

You can visit her Art gallery at www.faythe.fr

Milton Keynes UK
Ingram Content Group UK Ltd.
UKRC031159130324
439388UK00001B/4